INFORMANIA

Vampires

by Martin Jenkins

About This Book

Smitten by vampires? You're about to be! Here's everything you've ever wanted to know about these black-hearted bloodsuckers — and some things you've never even dreamt of!

It's midnight, and you are at the door of a Transylvanian castle. As it creaks open, a ghoulish figure beckons you inside saying, "I am Dracula, and I bid you welcome". Prepare to meet the scariest vampire ever, in my picture strip version of Bram Stoker's gripping novel!

Dracula and his friends may be creatures of fantasy, but there are animals out there that really do feed on blood. To find out more I set up the Vampire Investigation Project, and then put its top agents to work hunting down the chief offenders.

Section 3...page 45
A History of Bloodsucking

From the bloodthirsty demons of Babylonian mythology, to Vlad "the Impaler" Dracula – the history of vampirism is so mind-bogglingly murky that I've had to call on the learned Professor Harold von Blut to help sort the facts from the fantasy.

Section 4...page 65
Vampire Movies

Hundreds of vampire films – starring actors such as Bela Lugosi, Christopher Lee and Tom Cruise – have been made since the silent classic *Nosferatu* was first screened in 1922. Settle down for my Draculathon – twenty-four hours of the world's spookiest vampire movies.

Ready Reference...page 83

And finally, to tighten your grip on the facts, there's a Vampire Hunter's Survival Guide, a Glossary, and of course, an Index.

Martin Jenkins

About the Author

Martin Jenkins became hooked on vampires after seeing the 1922 silent movie *Nosferatu*. Since then he's watched dozens of other vampire movies and read countless books about these mythical monsters.

He's never come across a vampire himself, of course! But he has been attacked by plenty of real bloodsuckers, including giant mosquitoes in South America and leeches in Madagascar.

Martin is an expert on endangered species and, when he's not writing books for children, he spends his time working for conservation organizations such as the WorldWide Fund for Nature.

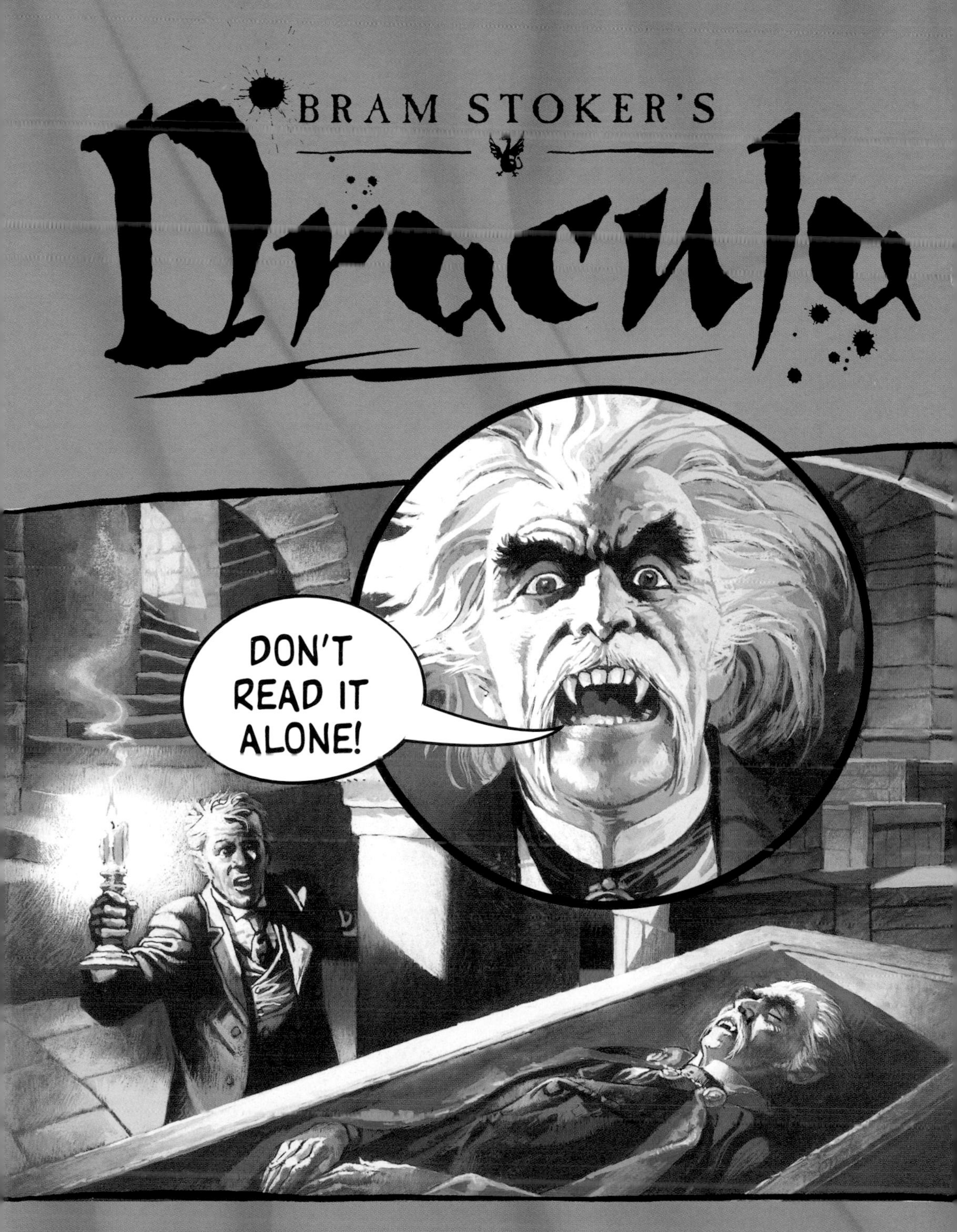

SPECIAL PICTURE-STRIP EDITION

The birth of a legend...

A tall cloaked figure bends over the sleeping girl as if to kiss her. But, no — his face hovers at her throat...

If you've ever read a book about vampires, or seen a movie, you'll know what happens next! What you may not know is that although bloodcurdling tales have been around for centuries, we really have one man to thank for the scariest vampire of all.

The man's name was Bram (short for Abraham) Stoker, and he was born in Ireland in 1847. He was ill for a long time when he was young, and his mother used to tell him stories to cheer him up. She particularly liked gruesome ones — a habit she evidently passed on to her son!

Bram grew up to work for the government in Dublin. But his real love was the theatre, and in 1878 he went to London to manage the Lyceum Theatre.

In his spare time Bram wrote stories, mostly adventure tales

and romances. But in 1890 he began work on something completely different — a book inspired by a nightmare in which he was attacked by three female vampires.

To turn this dream into as realistic a story as possible, Bram read everything he could lay his hands on about vampire myths and legends.

He decided that Transylvania (today part of Romania) would be the perfect place to set the beginning of his story, and quite soon he'd worked out most of the plot. But he still hadn't thought up a name for his main character or a title for his book.

Then Bram remembered reading about a bloodthirsty Romanian who lived in the 15th century and was called Vlad Dracula!

Bram Stoker's *Dracula* was published in 1897. It wasn't an instant bestseller, and it didn't make Bram's fortune, but over the past hundred years it has certainly earned him pride of place in the horror hall of fame!

BRAM STOKER, 1847–1912

Transylvania, eastern Europe
COUNT DRACULA HAS BOUGHT CARFAX HOUSE, A LARGE PROPERTY IN ENGLAND. A YOUNG SOLICITOR, JONATHAN HARKER, HAS BEEN SENT ABROAD TO THE COUNT'S CASTLE, WITH SALE DOCUMENTS FOR HIM TO SIGN.
IT IS LONG PAST MIDNIGHT WHEN JONATHAN ARRIVES AT CASTLE DRACULA.
I AM DRACULA, AND I BID YOU WELCOME, MR HARKER, TO MY HOUSE.
ENTER FREELY AND OF YOUR OWN WILL.
THE COUNT ASKS JONATHAN TO STAY FOR A WHILE, TO HELP HIM PREPARE FOR THE MOVE TO ENGLAND.

BUT AS THE DAYS GO BY, JONATHAN BEGINS TO THINK THERE'S SOMETHING RATHER PECULIAR ABOUT HIS HOST.
HUH? HOW COME I CAN'T SEE HIS REFLECTION IN MY MIRROR?

THE COUNT IS STRANGELY ABSENT DURING THE DAYTIME. AND THOUGH THEY MEET AT DINNER, JONATHAN NEVER SEES HIM EATING.
I HAVE DINED ALREADY.

BUT THAT'S NOT ALL. APART FROM THE TWO OF THEM, THE CASTLE SEEMS DESERTED, AND MOST OF THE DOORS ARE LOCKED...
EVEN THE OUTER ONES — JONATHAN IS A PRISONER.

THEN ONE NIGHT HE SEES SOMETHING TERRIFYING — A HUGE BAT-LIKE CREATURE CRAWLING DOWN THE CASTLE WALL.
GOD HELP ME — IT'S THE COUNT!

DETERMINED TO LEAVE THE CASTLE AS SOON AS POSSIBLE, JONATHAN HUNTS FOR A WAY OUT. HE FINDS AN UNLOCKED ROOM, BUT ONCE INSIDE A STRANGE FEELING COMES OVER HIM...
SO TIRED... MUST... LIE... DOWN...

NOT KNOWING IF HE IS DREAMING OR AWAKE, JONATHAN SEES THREE STRANGE WOMEN. ONE LEANS FORWARD AS IF TO KISS HIM...
WWHHHH???

SUDDENLY THE COUNT BURSTS IN, HIS EYES BLAZING WITH FURY.
LEAVE HIM! THIS MAN BELONGS TO ME!!

WHEN JONATHAN AWAKES,
HE IS BACK IN HIS
OWN ROOM — DID THE COUNT
CARRY HIM THERE OR WAS
IT ALL A DREAM?

GROWING EVER MORE
DESPERATE TO ESCAPE,
JONATHAN CONTINUES
HIS SEARCH. HE DISCOVERS
A WINDING STAIRCASE...

IT LEADS TO A CHAPEL PILED HIGH WITH WOODEN CHESTS.
THEY ARE ALL FILLED WITH EARTH — AND IN ONE
IS THE COUNT!

HORRIFIED BY HIS DISCOVERY, AND CERTAIN NOW THAT HIS
LIFE IS IN DANGER, JONATHAN FLEES TO HIS OWN ROOM.
ESCAPE SEEMS IMPOSSIBLE.

BUT THEN, A FEW DAYS LATER, JONATHAN REALIZES THAT
THE COUNT HAS LEFT THE CASTLE — TAKING ALL THE
WOODEN CHESTS WITH HIM.

England, some weeks later

BUT AS MINA RUSHES TOWARDS HER FRIEND,
THE MYSTERIOUS FIGURE VANISHES.

OVER THE NEXT FEW DAYS, MINA BECOMES INCREASINGLY CONCERNED ABOUT LUCY.

SHE NOTICES TWO MARKS, LIKE TINY BITES, ON HER FRIEND'S NECK. AND ONE NIGHT SHE FINDS LUCY SITTING UP IN BED ASLEEP, POINTING AT THE WINDOW.

MINA PEERS OUT INTO THE DARKNESS.

THEN LUCY DEVELOPS A MYSTERIOUS ILLNESS THAT MAKES HER GROW WEAKER AND WEAKER.

MINA IS WORRIED ABOUT JONATHAN, TOO.

AT LAST A LETTER ARRIVES. JONATHAN IS ALIVE, BUT HE'S IN A HOSPITAL ABROAD — HE WAS TAKEN ILL AFTER SCALING THE WALLS OF COUNT DRACULA'S CASTLE AND MAKING HIS ESCAPE.

MINA LEAVES AT ONCE, TO GO TO HIM AND BRING HIM HOME.

BUT SADLY, ALL VAN HELSING'S SKILL CANNOT SAVE LUCY, AND SHE DIES.

VAN HELSING BELIEVES THAT LUCY WAS ATTACKED BY A VAMPIRE AND HAS NOW BECOME ONE HERSELF. HE DECIDES TO KEEP WATCH NEAR HER TOMB, AND ASKS HER FIANCÉ, ARTHUR HOLMWOOD, AND HER FRIENDS, QUINCEY MORRIS AND JACK SEWARD, TO JOIN HIM.

ARTHUR HOLMWOOD

QUINCEY MORRIS

JACK SEWARD

TOWARDS DAWN, A SINISTER FORM MAKES ITS WAY THROUGH THE TREES TOWARDS THE TOMB.

THERE IS ONLY ONE THING THEY CAN DO FOR LUCY NOW...

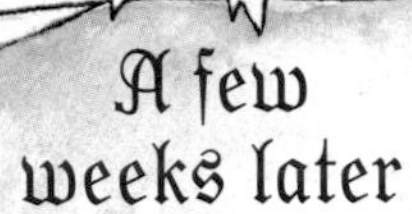

MINA AND JONATHAN HAVE RETURNED TO ENGLAND, AND VAN HELSING HAS VISITED THEM. HE HAS LEARNT OF JONATHAN'S NIGHTMARE STAY IN COUNT DRACULA'S CASTLE, AND OF THE ARRIVAL OF THE DEMETER WITH ITS STRANGE CARGO.

THE PROFESSOR ASKS JONATHAN AND MINA TO MEET WITH HIM AND LUCY'S OTHER FRIENDS, ARTHUR, QUINCEY AND JACK. THEY ALL GATHER AT JACK'S HOUSE NEAR LONDON.

THE NEXT DAY, THE MEN VISIT CARFAX HOUSE, HOPING THEY WILL FIND DRACULA THERE. THE CHESTS ARE IN THE CHAPEL.

THEY DECIDE TO TRACK DOWN THE MISSING BOXES. VAN HELSING SAYS HE'LL STAY WITH MINA. WITH DRACULA'S HOUSE SO CLOSE BY, SHE MAY BE IN DANGER.

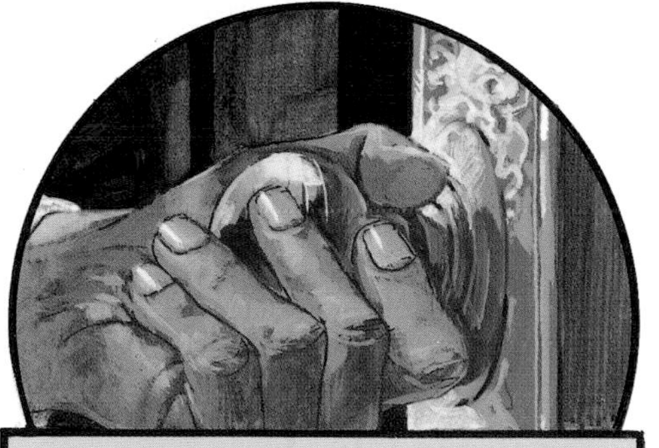

THAT EVENING VAN HELSING FINDS THE DOOR TO MINA'S ROOM LOCKED.

WITH THE OTHERS' HELP, HE BREAKS INTO THE ROOM. DRACULA IS INSIDE, FORCING MINA TO DRINK HIS BLOOD!

THE MEN BRANDISH CRUCIFIXES AND DRACULA VANISHES. THEN VAN HELSING PLACES A HOLY COMMUNION WAFER ON MINA'S FOREHEAD.
AAAAH!!!
THIS MAY HELP PROTECT HER AGAINST DRACULA.
BUT THE WAFER BURNS INTO MINA'S SKIN, SCARRING HER FOREHEAD.
WH-WHAT'S HAPPENING TO ME?
MY DEAR, THE SCAR SHOWS YOU'VE BEEN AFFECTED BY DRACULA'S BLOOD.
HE MUST BE DESTROYED IF WE ARE TO SAVE YOU FROM LUCY'S FATE.
BUT HOW CAN WE FIND HIM?
ATTACKING THE CHESTS WILL FORCE HIM INTO THE OPEN — HE'LL HAVE NOWHERE TO HIDE.
LEAVING MINA AT JACK'S HOUSE, THE MEN DESTROY THE CHESTS IN CARFAX HOUSE. THEN THEY RACE TO LONDON — THEY HAVE TRACED THE OTHER BOXES TO SEVERAL HOUSES THERE.

FINALLY THEY REACH THE LAST HOUSE, HOPING TO FIND THE REMAINING FEW BOXES.

OH, NO — ONE'S STILL MISSING!

JUST THEN THEY HEAR FOOTSTEPS . . .

DRACULA BURSTS IN! DEFIANTLY, THE MEN HOLD UP CRUCIFIXES. HE BACKS AWAY.

AND THROWS HIMSELF THROUGH THE WINDOW!

ONCE OUTSIDE, DRACULA TURNS TO TAUNT THEM . . .

YOU WILL BE SORRY YET, EACH ONE OF YOU. MY REVENGE HAS JUST BEGUN!

THEN HE VANISHES.

NOT KNOWING WHERE TO SEARCH NEXT, THE MEN RETURN TO MINA. LATER THAT NIGHT, SHE SUGGESTS A DARING PLAN TO THE PROFESSOR...
I FEEL LINKED TO DRACULA IN SOME WAY...
IF YOU HYPNOTIZE ME, I MAY BE ABLE TO SENSE WHERE HE IS.
WHERE ARE YOU? WHAT DO YOU HEAR?
LAPPING WATER... A CREAKING CHAIN...
VAN HELSING REALIZES THAT DRACULA IS ON BOARD A SHIP. THE COUNT MUST BE TRYING TO RETURN HOME BY SEA — AND HE MUST HAVE TAKEN THE LAST CHEST WITH HIM!
THE FRIENDS DECIDE TO CROSS EUROPE BY RAIL. IT WILL BE QUICKER, AND THEY MAY BE ABLE TO CATCH DRACULA BEFORE HE REACHES THE SAFETY OF HIS CASTLE.
TRANSYLVANIA
Castle Dracula
GALATZ
VARNA

VAN HELSING AND MINA ARE THE FIRST TO ARRIVE AT THE COUNT'S CASTLE. TOGETHER, THEY WATCH AND WAIT FOR THEIR FRIENDS.

AS JACK, ARTHUR, QUINCEY AND JONATHAN REACH THE HORSEMEN, A FIERCE FIGHT BREAKS OUT.

QUINCEY IS FATALLY WOUNDED...

BUT THE FRIENDS STILL WIN THEIR WAY TO THE CART.

THE SUN IS ALMOST SETTING WHEN JONATHAN AT LAST WRENCHES THE CHEST OPEN.

THE COUNT'S RED EYES ARE ABLAZE WITH HATRED...

BUT IN AN INSTANT, JONATHAN SLASHES DRACULA'S THROAT AND QUINCEY PLUNGES A KNIFE DEEP INTO THE MONSTER'S HEART.

AS DRACULA CRUMBLES INTO DUST, QUINCEY SINKS TO THE GROUND. HIS DYING WORDS ARE FOR MINA...

CASE STUDY NO. VIP/4

VAMPIRE INVESTIGATION PROJECT

MEMO TO: FIELD AGE

SUBJECT: THE MYSTE OF THE MAS

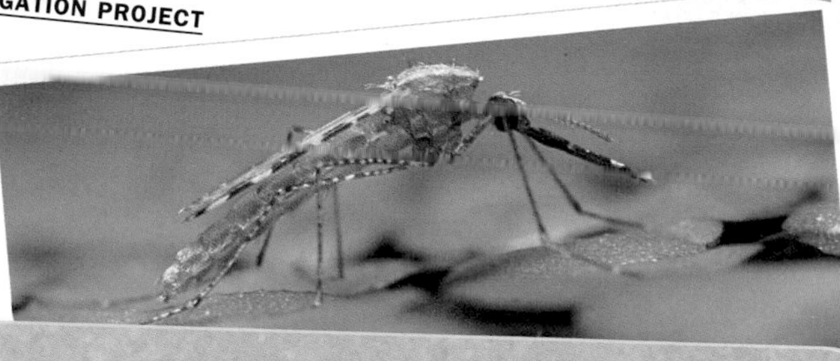

THE V FILES

Agents	Ian M. Dotti Sophia O. Smart
Project No.	145 – VIP
Objective	To discover the truth, however horrible, about animals that feed on blood!
IMPORTANT	Take a torch

CONFIDENTIAL ■ INFORMATION ■

VAMPIRE INVESTIGATION PROJECT

CODE NUMBER 136/17 BRE24 NM

AUTHORIZED BY Brian A. Thorne

Agent's name IAN M. DOTTI

TOP SECRET ✖ AUTHORIZED PERSONNEL ONLY ✖ TOP SECRET ✖ AUTHORIZED PERSONNEL ONLY

CONFIDENTIAL MEMO

TO: SPECIAL AGENT Sophia O. Smart
SUBJECT: THE VAMPIRE INVESTIGATION PROJECT

Here's the brief, Sophia. The boss wants us to find out whether there's any truth in all those vampire books and films — i.e., if there really is anything big out there that kills people by sucking out their blood. And by big, I mean big — man-sized (sorry, person-sized) and really scary.

Our field agent is Ian M. Dotti. He's keen, I'll give him that, but inexperienced, and I'm relying on you to write thorough case reports and maintain the project folder.

Give it your best shot, Sophia!

CASE STUDY NO. VIP/1

MEMO TO: FIELD AGENT Ian M. Dotti

SUBJECT: THE CURIOUS CASE OF THE CATTLE ATTACKERS

Here's your first case, Dotti. Get on to it quickly, and send your report back to H.Q. for Special Agent Smart to analyze.

ASSIGNMENT DETAILS:
Reports of night-time attacks on cattle, horses and even chickens have been sent in from South America. Blood has been found on the ground, and scurrying mice-like creatures have been seen. There are rumours of attacks on humans, too!

SPECIAL INSTRUCTIONS:
Fly to the Venezuelan capital, Caracas. Our local agent has hired a light plane to take you to the X-Brand Ranch in the central plains.

Good luck, Dotti — and don't take any unnecessary risks!

MY CASE NOTES by Field Agent I. M. Dotti

DAY 1

Have set up base camp in an area where I'm told there have been plenty of attacks. Plan to attract one of the creatures for capture by sleeping with my big toes sticking out of the tent.

Bait

DAY 5

Only result so far is cold feet. It's time for my back-up plan — will lie in wait tonight near some sleeping cattle.

DAY 6 — SUCCESS!!

Captured one of the creatures just before dawn — it was so bloated with blood it could scarcely fly. It's not a mouse, but A SMALL BAT!

LIVE SPECIMEN ENCLOSED

MUST REMEMBER TO TAKE MY CAMERA NEXT TIME!

FOR THE ATTENTION OF: Chief Officer B. A. Thorne

CASE REPORT No. 1

by Special Agent S. O. Smart

Field Agent Dotti has come up with the common vampire bat, a mouse-sized creature that rarely attacks humans and, despite its name, certainly cannot suck out enough blood to kill anyone. I have had its file sent over from archives, and I did a little additional research of my own — I must say, I find these bats fascinating!

A CLOSE SHAVE

Vampire bats usually land a short distance from their prey and then crawl carefully towards it, looking for a suitable feeding spot, such as an area of skin with few hairs or feathers.

After licking at the feeding spot to wet it, the bat uses its razor-sharp front teeth (see Pic. 1:1) to shave off any hairs or feathers and to slice away the skin.

FEEDING TIME

The vampire bat then uses its tongue rather like a straw to suck blood from the wound (see Pic. 1:2). As a rule the bat may feed for as long as 30 minutes, but only takes a few grammes of blood from its victim during this time.

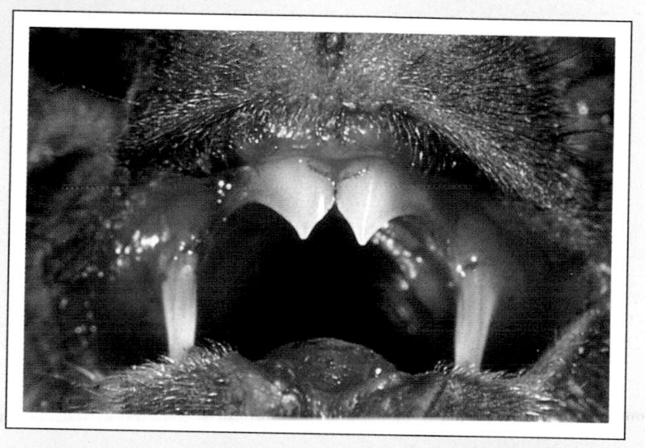

Picture 1:1 — teeth of the common vampire bat

Picture 1:2 — common vampire bat feeding on a chicken's leg

NAME: COMMON VAMPIRE BAT (Desmodus rotundus)

HABITAT: Central and South America, in woods and open plains.

DISTINGUISHING FEATURES: Greyish-brown mammal about 8 centimetres long. Extremely sharp triangular front teeth.

BEHAVIOUR: Is active at night, and only feeds on blood. Preys on horses, cattle, birds and other warm-blooded animals. Will sometimes attack sleeping humans.

RELATED ANIMALS: There are two other kinds of vampire bat, but they are quite rare and feed mainly on birds' blood. None of the other 900 or so species of bat is a bloodsucker.

PROPERTY OF
PLEASE RETURN
ARCHIVES DEPARTMENT

POSTSCRIPT

May I suggest that Dotti undergoes medical tests in case he was bitten while handling the specimen? Vampire bats can be dangerous to humans because they sometimes carry life-threatening diseases, such as rabies.

CASE STUDY No. VIP/2

MEMO TO: FIELD AGENT Ian M. Dotti

SUBJECT: THE STRANGE CASE OF THE BLEEDING BLUE-FOOTS

That bat stuff was interesting, Dotti, but it's not what we're looking for. They're too small, and it isn't their bloodsucking that harms people but the diseases they carry — how did your rabies test go, by the way?

Here's another lead. See what you can do with this one.

ASSIGNMENT DETAILS:

An anonymous informant has sent in a report of bloodsucking attacks on Isla Culpepper (one of the Galápagos Islands, off South America).

SPECIAL INSTRUCTIONS:

Make your way overland from Venezuela to Ecuador, and then get on a flight to Isla Baltra in the Galápagos. On arrival, join a tour boat going north to Isla Culpepper.

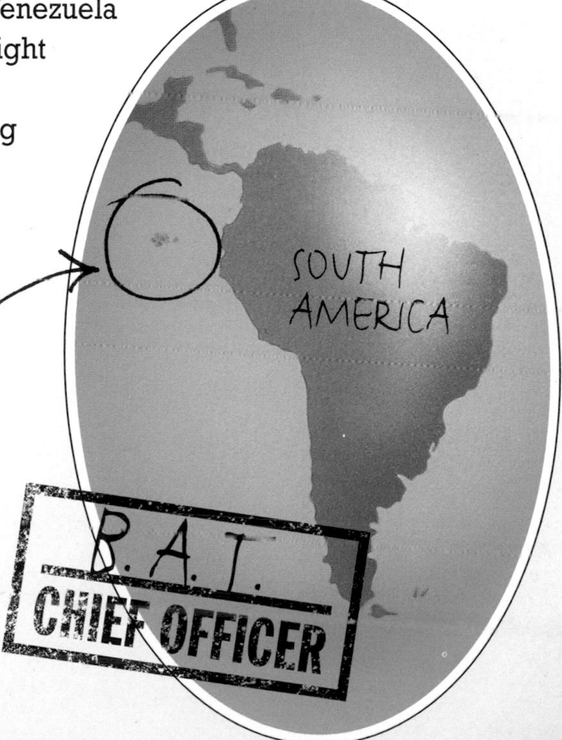

Be careful, Dotti — under no circumstances are you to use any part of yourself as bait this time!

MY CASE NOTES by Field Agent I. M. Dotti

DAY 1

Arrived this morning. Asked the tour guide if she knew anything about bloodsuckers, and it turns out they're attacking birds, not people!

DAY 2

Visited a colony of birds called blue-footed boobies. Several of them had BLEEDING TAILS. Saw a small bird pecking at one of the boobies.

DAY 6

Finally managed to buy some film for my camera. Hope the enclosed photographs are useful.

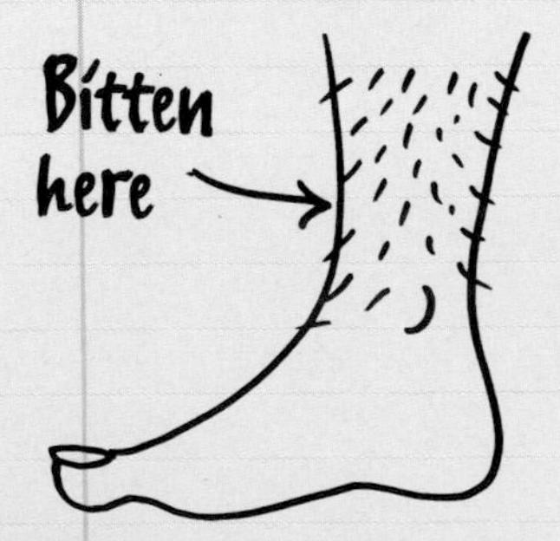

P.S. On my way to Ecuador I was attacked by a snake-like creature while wading through a river. The wound took ages to stop bleeding. Any idea what my attacker might be?

FOR THE ATTENTION OF: Chief Officer B. A. Thorne

CASE REPORT No. 2

by Special Agent S. O. Smart

Field Agent Dotti's small bird appears to be the sharp-beaked ground finch. Its bloodthirsty habits have only been recorded on a couple of islands, and it has never been known to attack people. It is not much of a lead.

CONCERNING DOTTI'S POSTSCRIPT

I have no knowledge of any bloodsucking snakes in South America, or indeed anywhere else in the world. Dotti's attacker remains a mystery.

NAME: SHARP-BEAKED GROUND FINCH (Geospiza difficilis)

HABITAT: Galápagos Islands.

DISTINGUISHING FEATURES: Dark-coloured bird, about 10 centimetres in length.

BEHAVIOUR: Usually feeds on seeds, birds' eggs, and small animals such as ticks. Drinks boobies' blood when its normal food is scarce. It pecks at the base of a booby's tail until a wound opens up and bleeds.

RELATED ANIMALS: There are about 1,000 finch species worldwide. Each has different feeding habits, but no other finch is known to feed on blood.

A BLOODY HISTORY

Leeches have been employed by healers for hundreds of years (see Pic. 3:2). They were used to remove blood from the body, because people once thought that illness could be caused either by having too much blood, or by having bad blood.

Picture 3:2 — medieval illustration of a woman applying leeches to her arm

USEFUL JUICES

This practice had mostly died out by the beginning of the 20th century. But after scientists discovered that some of the chemicals in leech saliva could be used as medicine, people started collecting leeches again, to extract the chemicals.

HELPING OUT IN HOSPITALS

Doctors started using live leeches once more in the 1970s — this time to help them with operations such as skin grafts. Nowadays, medicinal leeches are so rare that they are a protected species in most of the countries where they are found in the wild.

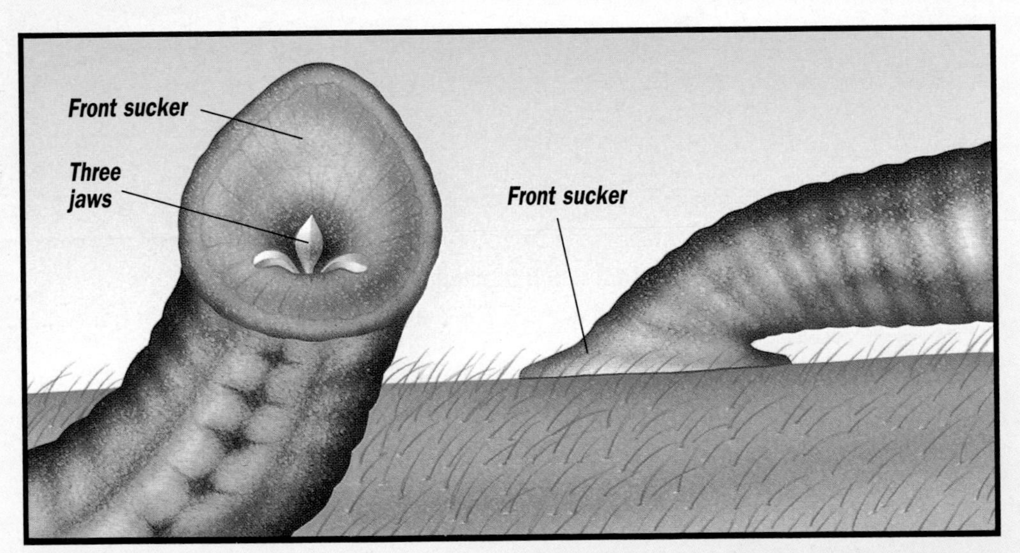

Picture 3:3 — the medicinal leech uses its jaws to cut through its victim's skin

NAME: EUROPEAN MEDICINAL LEECH (Hirudo medicinalis)

HABITAT: Europe, in freshwater ponds, streams and marshes.

DISTINGUISHING FEATURES: Flattened worm-like animal, up to 12 centimetres long. Blackish green coloured, with reddy-brown, orange and black spots. Has suckers at head and tail. Mouth has three jaws, each with about 100 tiny razor-sharp teeth.

BEHAVIOUR: After biting its victim (usually a frog or fish), the leech uses its suckers to attach itself. It feeds for about 20 minutes, and can drink as much as nine times its body weight in blood.

RELATED ANIMALS: Of the 500 or so leech species, about three-quarters are bloodsuckers. The rest feed on worms, snails and other small animals.

POSTSCRIPT

I now believe Dotti's mysterious South American attacker may have been a giant Amazonian horse-leech (Haementaria ghiliani). At about 50 centimetres long, this is the world's largest leech!

CASE STUDY NO. VIP/4

MEMO TO: FIELD AGENT Ian M. Dotti

SUBJECT: THE MYSTERIOUS CASE OF THE MASS MURDERERS

Really Dotti, what am I going to do with you? Your antics in the hospital nearly exposed the whole project. And not only is your leech harmless to humans, it's actually used to help them!

Here's another lead — don't make any more mistakes!

ASSIGNMENT DETAILS:

I've just heard something on the radio about one of the biggest killers of all — a "no-fleas" something-or-other which seems to be particularly deadly in Africa. I want you to get over there straight away.

SPECIAL INSTRUCTIONS:

Take the next available flight to the Tanzanian capital, Dar es Salaam. On arrival you are to locate an old colleague of mine, Dr Ibrahim Aziz. I'm sure he'll be able to help you find out what's going on.

And make sure you get some evidence this time!

MY CASE NOTES by Field Agent I. M. Dotti

DAY 1

Arrived in Dar es Salaam early this morning. Gee, it's hot.

My hotel!

DAY 8

Found Dr Aziz in his medical clinic. When I explained I was in pursuit of a bloodsucking mass-murderer called a "no-fleas" something-or-other, he rolled his eyes and started chuckling.

I'm still not sure what was so funny, but this time I'm bringing some EVIDENCE back with me! Dr Aziz assures me that whatever's inside the package will be helpful.

P.S. I realize it's only a small package, but perhaps it contains clues for me to follow up?

MUST REMEMBER TO TAKE TABLETS DOCTOR GAVE ME NEXT TIME!

This place is crawling with insects!

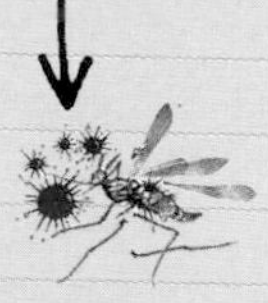

FOR THE ATTENTION OF: Chief Officer B. A. Thorne

CASE REPORT No. 4

by Special Agent S. O. Smart

Field Agent Dotti was extremely eager to be present when the package he brought back from Africa was opened in the laboratory. It contained a glass test tube. Unfortunately, in his attempts to assist, Dotti dropped the tube, and it smashed on impact with the floor.

SMALL BUT DEADLY

Having retrieved what appeared to be small pieces of an insect, I ascertained that the tube contained an Anopheles (pronounced "an–noh–fil–lees") mosquito (see Pic. 4:1).

This insect spreads malaria, a disease that kills as many as 2 million people a year worldwide, with the majority of deaths occurring in Africa.

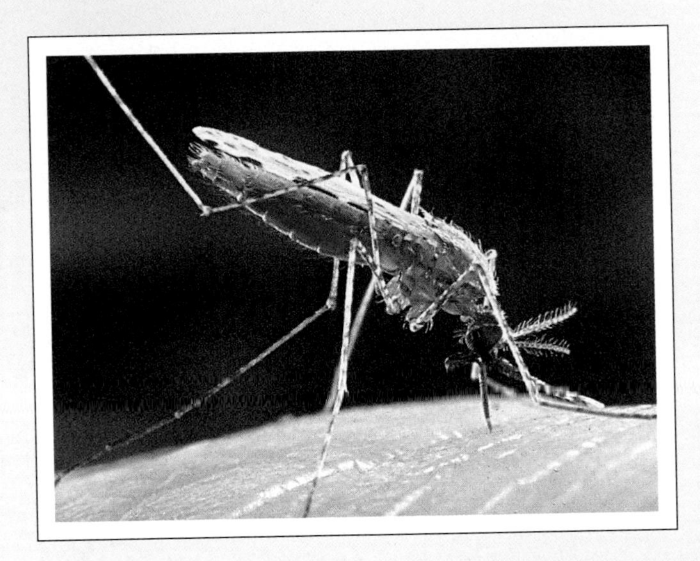

Picture 4:1 — an Anopheles mosquito feeding

HORRIBLE HITCH-HIKERS

Malaria is caused by a parasite (something that lives and feeds in or on another living creature). Malaria parasites spend part of their lives in the bodies of Anopheles mosquitoes, and part in the blood system of humans and other animals.

THE SPREAD OF MALARIA AMONG HUMANS

If a mosquito feeds on the blood of someone who has malaria, it sucks in some of the malaria parasites (see Pic. 4:2). These breed in the mosquito's stomach and the young enter its saliva. Then, when the mosquito bites another person, the parasites pass from its saliva to the new person's blood.

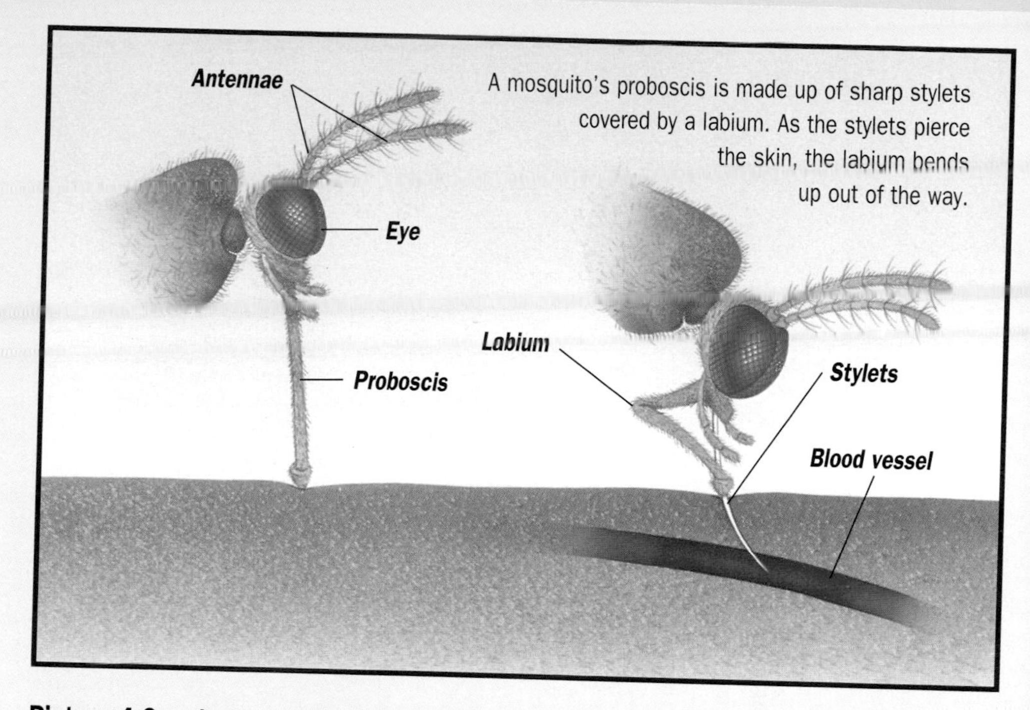

Picture 4:2 — how a mosquito pierces its victim's skin and feeds

MILLIONS OF MINIATURE KILLERS

Once the malaria parasites are inside a person's bloodstream they multiply rapidly (see Pic. 4:3), making millions of copies of themselves. This makes the victim extremely ill, and if proper medical treatment is unavailable, he or she may die.

Unfortunately, in the parts of the world where malaria is common, drugs to treat it are too expensive for many of the people who live there to afford — which is why the death rate from malaria is still so high.

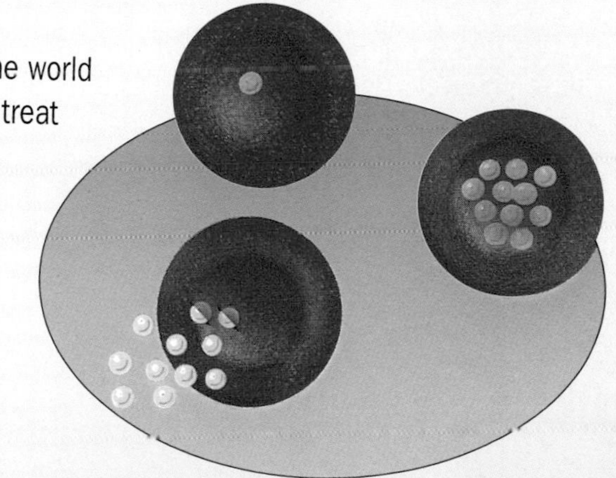

Picture 4:3 — malaria parasites multiply inside red blood cells, then burst out to invade more red blood cells

ANOTHER DEAD END

Although the Anopheles mosquito spreads malaria, it is the parasite that causes death. And no one could say that mosquitoes are big. Once again, we are no closer to fulfilling our project brief.

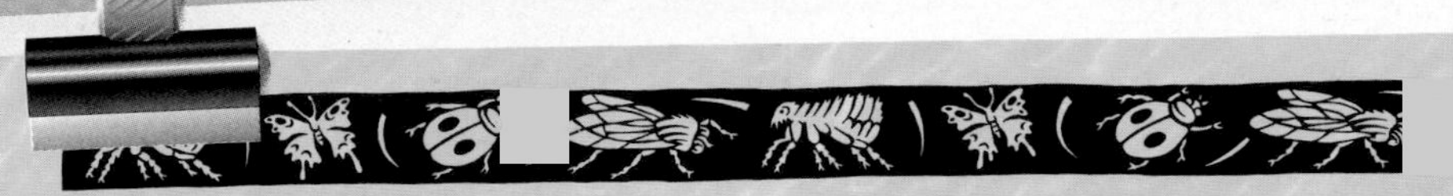

NAME: ANOPHELES MOSQUITOES (<u>Anopheles</u> species)

PLEASE RETURN
ARCHIVES DEPARTMENT

HABITAT: Warm wet places worldwide, but especially the wet tropical regions of Africa, South America and Asia.

DISTINGUISHING FEATURES: Insect about 0.5 centimetres long, with striped body.

BEHAVIOUR: Only adult females feed, usually during the cool of the evening and the early morning. They prey on a number of warm-blooded animals, including humans, sucking a tiny amount of blood through their proboscis.

RELATED ANIMALS: More than 1,500 mosquito species have been identified, including a few hundred Anopheles. Only about 24 of the Anopheles species carry the malaria parasites that infect humans.

<u>POSTSCRIPT</u>

I have included additional files on a number of other small bloodsucking animals for your information and interest.

I trust that Field Agent Dotti was taking his anti-malarial tablets during his visit to Tanzania?

NAME: DEER TICKS (Ixodes species)

HABITAT: Worldwide, in grass and shrub land.

DISTINGUISHING FEATURES: Brownish eight-legged oval animal, about 0.3 centimetres long.

BEHAVIOUR: Usually sucks blood from deer, cattle, humans and other warm-blooded animals. May carry illnesses such as Lyme disease.

RELATED ANIMALS: Ticks are related to spiders — they aren't insects. At least 200 deer tick species have been identified and named.

NAME: HEAD LOUSE (Pediculus humanus capitis)

HABITAT: Worldwide, in human head and body hair.

DISTINGUISHING FEATURES: Greyish-brown wingless insect, about 0.3 centimetres long.

BEHAVIOUR: Bites through skin and sucks blood. May carry serious diseases, including typhus.

RELATED ANIMALS: There are at least 400 species of sucking-louse.

NAME: HUMAN FLEA (Pulex irritans)

HABITAT: Worldwide, in the hair or fur of humans and other mammals.

DISTINGUISHING FEATURES: Brown wingless insect, about 0.4 centimetres long.

BEHAVIOUR: Sucks blood through its tiny proboscis. In some countries, may carry bubonic plague.

RELATED ANIMALS: Biologists think there are around 3,000 species of flea, all of them bloodsuckers that feed on mammals or birds.

NAME: TSETSE FLIES (Glossina species)

HABITAT: Africa, in areas with plenty of trees or shrubs.

DISTINGUISHING FEATURES: Yellowish, brown or grey insect, up to 1.3 centimetres long.

BEHAVIOUR: Mainly attacks large mammals, including cattle and humans. Sucks blood through its proboscis. Carries parasites that cause dangerous diseases, including sleeping sickness, in humans.

RELATED ANIMALS: There are about 20 tsetse fly species, all bloodsuckers.

CONFIDENTIAL MEMO

MEMO TO: SPECIAL AGENT Sophia O. Smart
SUBJECT: VAMPIRE INVESTIGATION PROJECT

Oh dear, oh dear. This insect stuff is fascinating, but it just isn't getting us anywhere. The boss told us to track down BIG bloodsuckers, yet every one of Dotti's animals seems to be smaller than the last one!

I'm beginning to despair of Dotti — it's looking like time to give him the push and find someone new. I'm sending him on holiday while I make my mind up.

Brian
CHIEF OFFICER

ROYALS UNDER ATTACK!!!!

SPECIAL REPORT by Field Agent I. M. Dotti

I know I'm supposed to be taking a holiday, but I'm sure this is OUR BIG BREAK!

I've heard that the British Royal Family is under threat from a huge BLOODSUCKING FISH!

APPARENTLY, IT'S ALREADY KILLED TWO OF THEM!!

I haven't got many details yet, but it all sounds really horrible. I'm going to try to find out what's going on — I'll keep you posted.

the British Royal Family

FOR THE ATTENTION OF: Chief Officer B. A. Thorne

CASE REPORT No. 5

by Special Agent S. O. Smart

I am sorry to hear about Field Agent Dotti's arrest at Buckingham Palace. Apparently, he was on the trail of a bloodsucking fish known as the river lamprey, but I'm afraid that, once again, he has the wrong end of the stick.

THE FOOD OF KINGS

Lampreys were once considered a great delicacy, and that is where the British Royal Family comes in — King John (1199–1216) and King Henry IV (1399–1413) are said to have been so fond of lampreys that they died after eating too many of them.

NAME: RIVER LAMPREY (Lampetra fluviatilis)

HABITAT: W. Europe, in rivers and shallow seawater.

DISTINGUISHING FEATURES: Tubular fish up to 40 centimetres long. Its tongue and mouth are lined with rows of small pointed teeth.

BEHAVIOUR: Preys on other fish, using its teeth to rasp through its victim's scales and skin, so it can suck out the blood and other body juices.

RELATED ANIMALS: There are about 40 species of lamprey, but although most are bloodsuckers, none of them attacks humans.

CONFIDENTIAL MEMO

TO: SPECIAL AGENT Sophia O. Smart
SUBJECT: VAMPIRE INVESTIGATION PROJECT

Dotti really has blown it this time. Some scientific bigwigs heard about his arrest and contacted the boss. They told her that there really aren't any big animals that kill people by bloodsucking – and certainly nothing like the vampires in books and movies.

The project's been cancelled. Dotti's been sacked, and we're being assigned to another department. All that's left is for you to hide this file at the back of a dark dusty cupboard. – somewhere NO ONE will EVER find it!

Brian

Harold von Blut
VAMPIRES
The Gory Story
Miss Millie von Blut
23 Silverthorne Way
CASTLEFORD
OCT 31

Professor Harold von Blut

The Black House, Stakeheart Lane, Much-Howling-in-the-Marsh

Dear Millie,

How lovely to have a letter from you. So, you've actually read Bram Stoker's DRACULA, have you? It's one of my favourite books, even if it is a bit long, not to say rather heavy going in places.

"Do vampires really exist?" you ask. The short answer is "No, of course not!" But I thought the enclosed might help to explain where the whole idea came from — and make a nice birthday present at the same time.

It's a little booklet I wrote for my local school, to show how people the world over have believed in vampires for centuries — despite the fact that there's never been a single shred of evidence to prove that they exist!

Happy birthday, and don't have too many nightmares!

With much love,

Uncle Harry
XXX

CHAPTER ONE

The Birth of the Bloodsucker

The history of horror dates back at least 5,000 years, to a time when people called the Babylonians lived beside the Euphrates River (in the region now known as Iraq).

It was the Babylonians who dreamt up the first spooky bloodsucker that anyone knows about — a female demon called *Lilitu*, who seems to have looked like a normal woman, but had the unpleasant habit of feasting on the blood of babies.

Freaky Greeks

A thousand or so years later, the Ancient Greeks were frightening themselves silly with stories of female demons called *Lamiae*. These monsters would apparently take their eyes out to rest when exhausted after a long night's bloodsucking!

Raving Romans

The *Striges* came along in Roman times. They had the head of a woman and the body of a bird. And guess what — like the Babylonians' *Lilitu*, they were particularly fond of the blood of babies and young children (and especially the ones that cried a lot).

CHAPTER FOUR

Grave Possibilities

Despite William's best efforts, tales of the undead weren't that common in western Europe. But things were a bit different in eastern and central Europe – the place seems to have been crawling with gruesome ghouls. Here's a selection!

- **Name:** ***NACHZEHRER*** *(Say nack-zee-rer)*
- **Distribution:** Silesia and Bavaria (today part of Poland and Germany)
- **Appearance:** TATTY! Started off as a fairly normal corpse, but with one eye open.
- **Behaviour:** Chewed its own grave shroud, then ate itself (starting at hands and feet), thereby making any living relatives waste away and die. Usually stayed in its grave, but might leave, taking the form of a BLOODSUCKING PIG!!

- **Name: *STRIGOI***
  (*Say strih-goy)*
- **Distribution:** Romania
- **Appearance:** SHOCKING!
  A corpse with two hearts.
- **Behaviour:** Preferred to drink milk, but if this ran out would suck blood. Normally attacked animals, but might go for people on the night before St Andrew's feast day (13th December for Orthodox Christians, but 30th November for others).

- **Name: *VRYKOLAKAS***
  (*Say vree-koe-la-kass)*
- **Distribution:** Greece and Macedonia
- **Appearance:** MOULDY!
  Usually a plump smelly corpse.
- **Behaviour:** Some would enter homes at night to smash things and generally make a nuisance of themselves. Others would knock on doors and call out the name of someone living inside. If that person answered, the *Vrykolakas* would return later and suffocate them by sitting on their chest.

CHAPTER FIVE

The First Vampires

By the late 17th century, creepy stories from eastern Europe had begun to reach big cities like Paris and London.

Poor Peter

But it wasn't until 1725 that the first "vampire" came along — or at least the first person to be called one in an official report. His name was Peter Plogojowitz, and he lived in the Serbian village of Kisilova.

Seriously sick

The trouble began a few weeks after Peter's death in 1725. Nine of his fellow villagers suddenly died of a mysterious illness — but not before claiming that Plogojowitz had visited them during the night and tried to kill them.

The remaining villagers were convinced that Plogojowitz had become a vampire. So they dug his body up, thrust a sharpened stake through his heart, and burnt the corpse!

Fanning the flames

Peter's story caused a bit of a stir, but even worse was to follow.

In 1732, an Austrian army medical officer called Johannes Flückinger also wrote a report. This one covered his investigation into what appeared to be a positive epidemic of vampirism in another Serbian village, Medvegia.

Hay fever

The whole sorry tale had begun back in 1727, when a villager called Arnod Paole died after falling from a hay wagon. It wasn't long before some of his fellow villagers began claiming that Paole was plaguing them at night. Then four of them suddenly fell ill and died, and other villagers said their animals had been attacked.

Here, in Flückinger's own words, is what the people of Medvegia did about Paole — but be warned, it's pretty strong stuff.

Flückinger's Report

"They dug up this Arnod Paole...and they found that... fresh blood had flowed from his eyes, nose, mouth and ears. The shirt, the covering, and the coffin were completely bloody. The old nails on his hands and feet, along with the skin, had fallen off, and new ones had grown. And since they saw from this that he was a true vampire, they drove a stake through his heart...whereby he gave an audible groan and bled copiously. Thereupon they burned the body the same day to ashes and threw these into the grave."

The calm before the storm

It was all quiet on the vampire front in Medvegia for a while...

then, in 1731, no fewer than seventeen villagers died within the space of a few weeks!

You are what you eat

This time, the people of Medvegia claimed that various villagers had become vampires after eating meat from the animals Paole was supposed to have attacked back in 1727.

Off with their heads!

Flückinger watched as all seventeen bodies were dug up. Twelve looked just like Paole's corpse had — oozing fresh blood, new fingernails...they had to be vampires!

Once again, they were dealt with pretty thoroughly. After their heads were cut off, the corpses were burnt and the ashes thrown in the river.

Seeing is believing

Flückinger was convinced he'd seen real vampires — but had he? Take a look opposite at what a modern-day doctor has to say about Arnod Paole's corpse, and you'll see that we now have perfectly reasonable explanations for all those mysterious signs of "vampirism"!

So why were Paole and all the other Serbian "vampires" turned into something sinister?

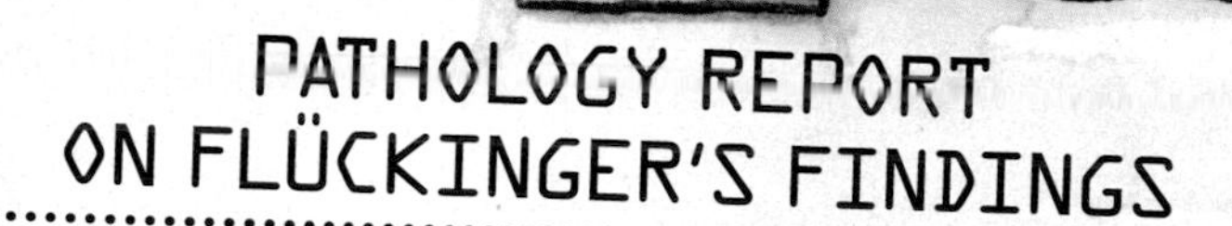

PATHOLOGY REPORT ON FLÜCKINGER'S FINDINGS

Flückinger's "signs of vampirism" were nothing of the sort — his report was just a fairly accurate description of what a corpse might look like a few weeks after it had been buried.

What Flückinger interpreted as "fresh blood" would have been a mixture of the reddish liquid produced as a corpse starts to rot, and reliquefied blood (blood usually sets after death, but can become runny again later).

It is common for people's nails and hair to grow a bit after they die, and the skin often comes loose and slips, showing what looks like new skin underneath.

Gases are also given off as bodies decompose — Arnod Paole's groan was probably caused by gases escaping from his body as it was punctured by the stake.

Don't blame me!

The answer is probably quite simple. If lots of people (or cattle) in your village started dying, and you couldn't think why, then you might start looking for someone to blame.

And who better than someone who'd just died, and who'd been rather unpopular or even a bit odd when they were alive!

CHAPTER SIX

Vampires in the News

Back in the 18th century, however, Flückinger's report was taken seriously, and versions of it were soon causing a sensation in newspapers all over Europe.

Vampire-mania

Suddenly everyone went vampire-mad. More and more accounts of people digging up "vampires" in eastern Europe appeared. Arguments raged about the sort of things these creatures might do.

Many learned articles and books were written on the subject. The longest and most famous was published in 1746, and was written by a French monk called Dom Augustin Calmet.

Although Dom Calmet had collected together a massive amount of information on vampirism, he didn't have an explanation for it. He did take the whole thing seriously, though, and he truly believed that something strange was going on.

Stuff and nonsense

But not everyone was taken in, and that splendid French historian and thinker Voltaire was one of the loudest critics of the whole business. He thought it was preposterous rubbish and said that if vampires really existed, how come they never turned up in places like London or Paris!

Literary revival

Towards the end of the 18th century things calmed down a bit, and stories about "real-life" vampires became few and far between.

But although the subject was dead, it wasn't buried — vampires were about to find a new lease of life in poems and novels.

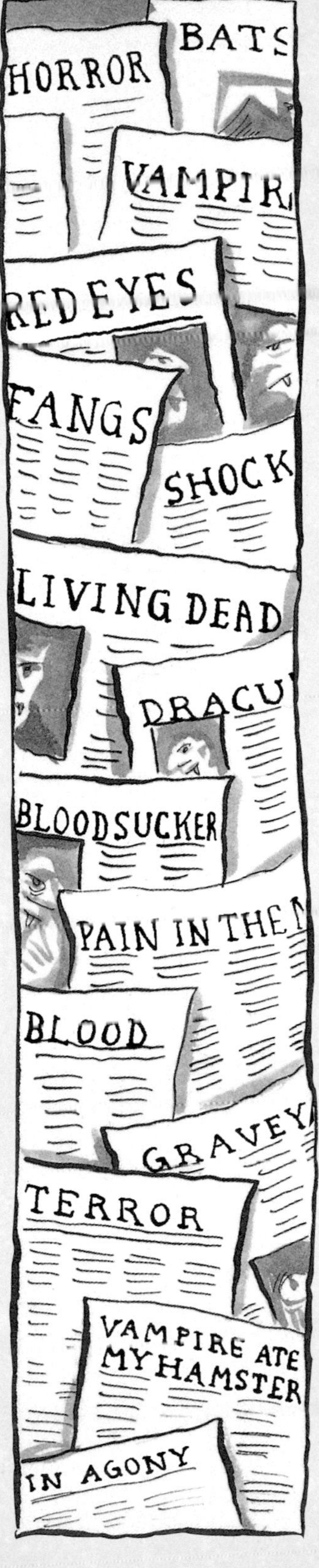

CHAPTER SEVEN

A Passion for Vampires

Poems with vampires in them started appearing in the 18th century, but the first fictional stories weren't written until the early 19th century.

The British poet Lord Byron began one of the very first in 1816, during the same weekend that Mary Shelley invented Frankenstein — but that's another story!

It's a steal!

Byron never finished his story. Instead, his secretary, John Polidori, stole the idea and turned it into *The Vampyre; A Tale*, published in 1819.

Polidori's vampire was called Lord Ruthven, and he looked an awful lot like Byron, whom Polidori loathed.

Light of my life

Ruthven spends a fair bit of time feasting on young maidens' blood before he's killed off... only he isn't, of course! Moonlight falls on his body and he revives, to carry on with his dastardly deeds!

A noble tradition

Suddenly, vampires were all the rage again. Only this time, like Lord Ruthven, they had to be tall, thin and aristocratic — quite unlike the earlier, "real-life" vampires, who were usually described as short, fat peasants.

And so, in the 1840s, along came Sir Francis Varney (who as it happens was the first vampire to have fangs). *Varney the Vampire* was published in weekly episodes, and Varney's adventures went on and on and on — for 220 chapters and 868 pages!

Fang-tastic?

Like all good vampires, Varney was practically indestructible. People kept killing him off, but every time they'd carelessly leave his body where the Moon's cold rays would fall on it, and he'd revive to terrorize a few more damsels in distress.

In the end even his biggest fans began to get bored, and Varney's creator (James Malcolm Rymer) was forced to make him commit suicide by jumping into the crater of Mount Vesuvius (a volcano near the Italian city of Naples).

CHAPTER EIGHT

Evil Women

That wasn't the end of vampires, of course, and in 1872 the Irish writer Sheridan Le Fanu gave the whole business a new twist by writing a short story about a female aristocratic vampire, whom he called Carmilla.

A friend in need?

In the story, Carmilla appears to be a beautiful (if strange) young woman, who pretends to befriend another young woman, called Laura.

But Carmilla is really a 200 year-old vampire countess, and what she's actually after is Laura's blood!

A real horror

Le Fanu's story was almost certainly inspired by the life of a real Hungarian countess called Erzebet Báthory.

Rather disappointingly perhaps, no one ever actually thought the Countess was a vampire. All the same, she was a dreadfully wicked woman.

She was born in 1560, and grew up to marry a Count Ferenc Nadasdy. But although the Countess was said to be very beautiful, the Count seems to have been more interested in going off to war than in spending time at home with her.

Hideous habits

The Countess must have got bored while her husband was away, because she turned extremely nasty. She became convinced that drinking and bathing in the blood of girls would help keep her young and beautiful.

Her servants lured village girls to the castle by saying they were needed as maids. In fact, they were kept prisoner in the dungeons and then horribly murdered.

Not surprisingly, the local people became suspicious about the girls' fate. Then, in 1610, the grizzly truth was discovered.

Head countess

To this day, nobody knows exactly how many girls the Countess killed. Some say 50, others, 600.

Revenge was swift. The castle servants were executed, and the Countess was locked away until her death in 1614.

A life in show business

The Countess and Carmilla live on, though — in the movies.

So the next time you see a vampire film, watch out for shifty young women in nightdresses. They'll probably turn out to be age-old monsters on the lookout for fresh supplies of human blood — to keep themselves forever youthful!

CHAPTER NINE

The Wicked Count

The most famous vampire of all time has to be Dracula. This evil Transylvanian count was the creation of Irishman Bram Stoker, whose story about him was published in 1897.

Like Le Fanu, Stoker was inspired by a real-life historical figure — a certain Romanian who went by the name of Vlad Dracula or Vlad Tepes.

Vlad the bad

The real Vlad Dracula was ruler of a part of Romania called Wallachia (which is actually quite a long way from Transylvania).

He was born in 1431 and inherited one of his names from his father, who was called Vlad Dracul. Dracula just means "son of Dracul", and Dracul means "devil" or "dragon" in Romanian.

Making a point

Although, like Countess Báthory, the real-life Dracula wasn't ever thought to have been a vampire, he did have some pretty unpleasant habits.

His favourite occupation seems to have been killing his enemies by impaling (or sticking) them on stakes. And that's how he got his other name — Vlad Tepes, which means Vlad the Impaler.

Vlad certainly had plenty of enemies. He spent most of his life fighting the Turks (who wanted to include Romania in their empire), or the Hungarians (who also had their eyes on Romania).

And in between, he found time to rebuild a ruined castle and to

massacre any of his subjects who annoyed him (evidently quite a few of them). He was finally killed in battle in 1476.

Something old, and something new

In some ways, Bram Stoker's Count Dracula was just like the vampires in earlier stories — he was, after all, tall, slim and aristocratic.

But in others he was quite different. Dracula was the first fictional vampire to come from eastern Europe, where all those "real-life" vampires were supposed to have come from back in the 18th century.

He was also the first vampire whose reflection didn't appear in mirrors, as well as the first to regularly turn into a bat.

There had been vampires who'd turned into animals before, but none of them ever seems to have fancied being a bat!

CHAPTER TEN

The Thoroughly Modern Vampire

These days, of course, it's pretty much unthinkable to have a vampire that doesn't transform itself into a bat whenever the mood takes it, or that can see its reflection in a mirror.

Bigger and better?

Vampires have changed in other ways since Bram Stoker's day, though. For a start, they're now mostly found in movies, not books.

Their fangs have grown a lot, too, and all that stuff about vampires being destroyed by the Sun's rays was invented by film directors — in Stoker's novel Dracula tends to rest in one of his boxes during the day, but there's no suggestion that sunlight might harm him.

It's all make-believe...

In the end, we all know deep down that vampires are just figments of people's imaginations.

Even so, on a dark night with the wind howling, it's easy to convince yourself that a sinister cloaked figure with red eyes and long sharp fangs really is hovering outside your bedroom window — and that it's just waiting for you to fall asleep...

THE WORLD'S TOP VAMPIRE FILMS,
A 24-HOUR TV SPECTACULAR

Welcome, horror fans...

to the Midnight Channel's DRACULATHON — twenty-four hours of television devoted to non-stop blood-curdling vampire viewing!

With more than 1,000 vampire films and TV programmes made to date, deciding which ones to choose for our Draculathon hasn't been easy.

We hope you enjoy our selection — it's got some of the best films and some of the very worst, some of the scariest and even some of the funniest.

We've given pride of place to the most famous vampire of them all — Count Dracula.

The evil Transylvanian has appeared in well over

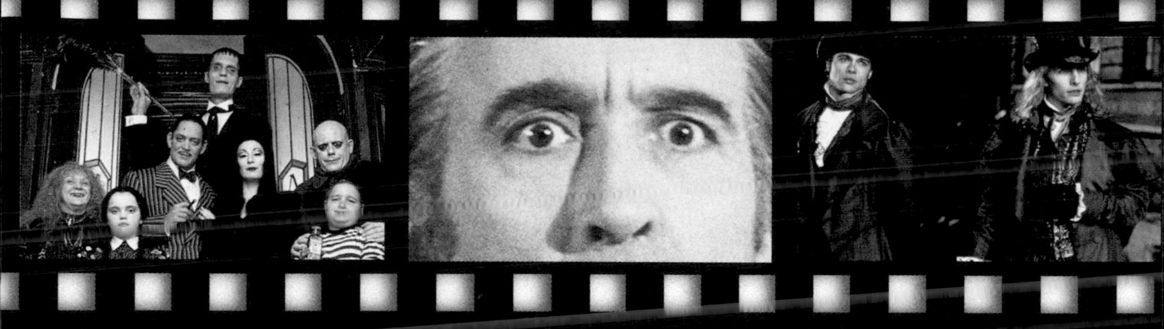

a hundred movies, but only about a dozen are at all closely based on Bram Stoker's original story.

We've picked four of them — *Nosferatu* (1922), *Dracula* (1931), *Dracula* (1958), and *Bram Stoker's Dracula* (1992).

Turn the page for a listings guide. To help you make your choice and plan your viewing, each film and TV programme has been given a rating.

Read on — for movie reviews, and special features on star vampire actors and actresses.

Then settle down in your favourite chair and bolt the door — who knows what fiendish bloodsuckers you'll be keeping at bay!

Listings Guide

12.00am–1.24am
NOSFERATU
d. F.W. Murnau, Germany, r. 1922, b/w, 84 min.

1.35am–3.00am
DRACULA
d. Tod Browning, USA, r. 1931, b/w, 85 min.

3.10am–4.20am
VAMPYR
d. Carl Theodor Dreyer, Germany, r. 1932, b/w, about 70 min. (originally 83 min.)

4.35am–5.57am
DRACULA
d. Terence Fisher, UK, r. 1958, col., 82 min.

Christopher Lee stars in Dracula at 4.35am

Billy the Kid vs Dracula at 9.20am

Abbreviations

b/w	=	black and white
col.	=	colour
d.	=	director
min.	=	minutes
r.	=	released (date first shown in country of origin)

6.10am–7.29am
PLAN 9 FROM OUTER SPACE
d. Edward Wood, USA, r. 1959, b/w, 79 min.

7.40am–9.05am
THE BRIDES OF DRACULA
d. Terence Fisher, UK, r. 1960, col., 85 min.

9.20am–10.49am
BILLY THE KID VS DRACULA
d. William Beaudine, USA, r. 1965, col., 89 min.

11.00am–12.30pm
DRACULA PRINCE OF DARKNESS
d. Terence Fisher, UK, r. 1966, col., 90 min.

12.45pm–2.32pm
DANCE OF THE VAMPIRES
d. Roman Polanski, UK/USA, r. 1967, col., 107 min.

2.45pm–4.15pm
THE MUNSTERS
Kayro Vue/Universal/CBS-TV, US, 1964–1966, b/w, 30-min. episodes

4.30pm–5.30pm
DARK SHADOWS
Dan Curtis/ABC-TV, USA, 1966–1971, col., 30-min. episodes

5.45pm–6.58pm
THE NIGHT STALKER
d. John Llewellyn Moxey, Dan Curtis/ABC-TV, USA, 1972, col., 73 min.

7.10pm–7.30pm
COUNT DUCKULA
Cosgrave Hall, UK, 1988, col. cartoon, 5-min. episodes

7.40pm–9.43pm
BRAM STOKER'S DRACULA
d. F. Ford Coppola, USA, r. 1992, col., 123 min.

10.00pm–12.01am
INTERVIEW WITH THE VAMPIRE
d. Neil Jordan, USA, r. 1994, col., 121 min.

Key to Ratings

Terrific
Toothsome
Tasty
Tolerable
Terrible, but fun

The Graveyard Shift

Our programmes kick off at midnight, the witching hour, with some of the very first vampire films ever made. These films may be ancient and they're all black-and-white, but be warned — they still have the power to chill the blood!

12.00am–1.24am

NOSFERATU (1922)

Extremely spooky silent movie, whose title comes from an old German word for a vampire.

▲ ***The monstrous Max Schreck in Nosferatu***

This was the first film to be based on Bram Stoker's novel. But although its plot is similar to that of the book, the characters' names are different, and much of the story is set in Germany, not England.

Count Dracula is named Count Orlok, for example, and he's visited in his castle by a young German solicitor, whose name is Thomas Hutter.

Orlok attacks Ellen, Thomas' wife, and is eventually destroyed when the morning sun shines on him while he's feasting on her blood. (In the novel, of course, the Count is polished off with knives.)

A famous German actor called Max Schreck — whose surname means "fright" or "terror" in German — created the scariest, ugliest Count in the entire history of the movies. A must see!

Fancy That

The idea that a vampire can be destroyed by sunlight first surfaced in *Nosferatu.*

▶ ***Bela Lugosi welcomes his victims with open arms***

1.35am–3.00am

DRACULA (1931)

The first talkie based on Bram Stoker's novel stars Bela Lugosi (see p. 74) as the demon Count.

The film is fairly faithful to the plot of the novel, although Dracula is destroyed — off-screen, unfortunately — not by Jonathan Harker, but by Van Helsing.

The London scenes are rather slow and boring, but the ones set in Transylvania are spooky and very scary!

🦇🦇🦇

3.10am–4.20am

VAMPYR (1932)

This eerie movie is based in part on Sheridan Le Fanu's short story "Carmilla" (see p. 60).

The action really gets going after Leone, a Transylvanian lord's daughter, is found in the grounds of her home at night. She's lost a lot of blood and a strange old woman is hovering over her body.

The film's hero, David Gray, comes to realize that the old woman is a vampire. He eventually destroys her (with a servant's help) by staking her with an iron pole.

A very creepy and rather wonderful movie.

🦇🦇🦇🦇

Dread at Dawn

Not many vampire movies were made during the 1940s and 1950s, but just when audiences thought it was safe to go back in the cinema . . . Dracula returned from the grave to haunt another generation of movie-goers!

4.35am–5.57am

DRACULA (1958)

In this, the first colour version of Stoker's novel, Christopher Lee (see p. 75) plays the Count, and Peter Cushing is Van Helsing.

The film's climax differs from that of the novel, but is still thrilling — Dracula crumbles to dust after Van Helsing uses a cross made from two candlesticks to force him into the sunlight.

One of the best Dracula films ever made, and with lots of blood and gore, still chilling after all these years!

Fancy That

Christopher Lee wore coloured contact lenses in *Dracula,* to turn his eyes a vampiric shade of red.

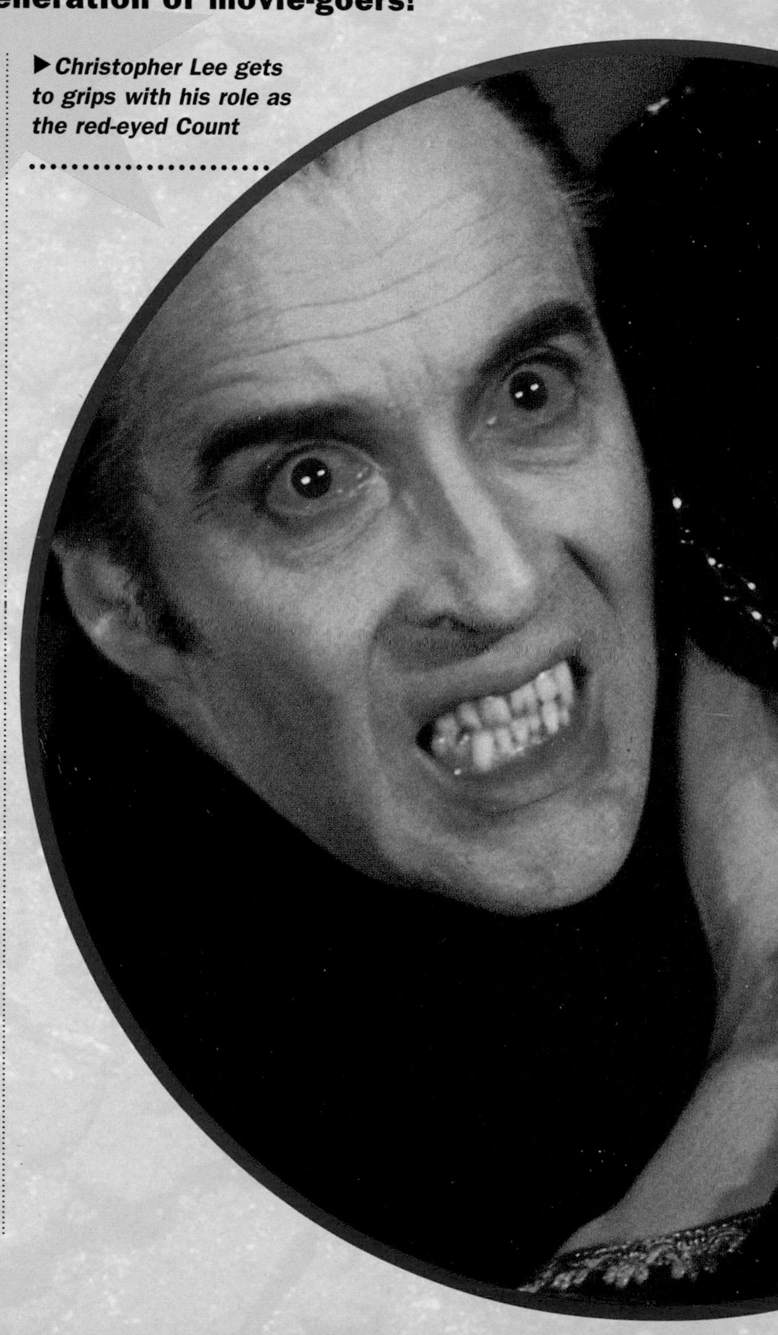

▶ ***Christopher Lee gets to grips with his role as the red-eyed Count***

6.10am–7.29am

PLAN 9 FROM OUTER SPACE (1959)

A very silly story about a pair of aliens trying (unsuccessfully) to take over the Earth — with the help of vampires and an army of corpses raised from their graves. Even the sets are wobbly — in one scene, a cardboard tombstone actually falls over! Don't miss it!

▲ ***Bat attack! Peter Cushing in The Brides of Dracula***

7.40am–9.05am

THE BRIDES OF DRACULA (1960)

Despite its title, this film doesn't feature Dracula. Instead, it gives him a vampire disciple, Baron Meinster, who's kept locked up by his mother until a local schoolteacher (who's unaware of his nasty habits) frees him!

Meinster terrorizes the schoolgirls until he's destroyed by the fearless Van Helsing, again played by Peter Cushing.

The film wasn't a great success when it first came out, as audiences were expecting to see Dracula and were disappointed when he didn't appear. But it's actually rather good!

▲ ***David Peel bares his fangs as Baron Meinster***

LORDS OF THE NIGHT

Of all the actors who've played Dracula over the years, only a few have really made their mark. Meet three of the men who've helped shape our view of the perfect vampire.

▼ *The elegant Bela Lugosi*

BELA LUGOSI

★ ***(1882–1956)*** ★

Hungarian-born Bela Lugosi was the first actor to utter the immortal line "I am Dracula" on the silver screen (in the 1931 film *Dracula*). He emigrated to America in 1920, and his starring role in *Dracula* was followed by parts in numerous other horror movies, including five as a vampire.

Lugosi's Count Dracula was elegant and extremely polite, but still deadly — despite not having any fangs.

JOHN CARRADINE

★ ***(1906–1988)*** ★

Tall, thin American actor John Carradine made a ghoulish and sinister vampire. When acting the part he usually had a moustache — and often a top hat — but like Lugosi, he was fangless.

Carradine played Dracula nine times in all — more often than any other actor, apart from Christopher Lee.

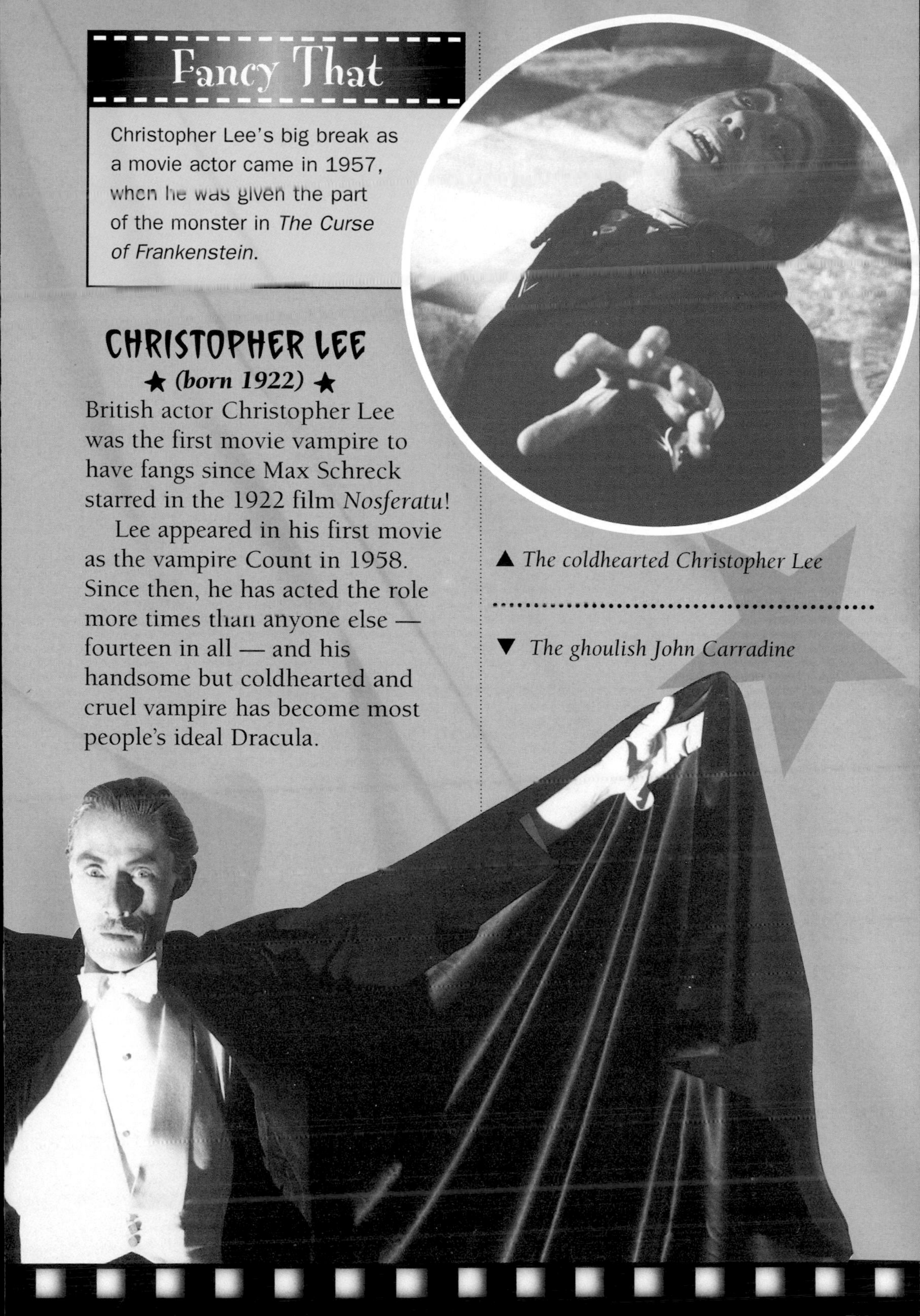

Fancy That

Christopher Lee's big break as a movie actor came in 1957, when he was given the part of the monster in *The Curse of Frankenstein*.

CHRISTOPHER LEE

★ (born 1922) ★

British actor Christopher Lee was the first movie vampire to have fangs since Max Schreck starred in the 1922 film *Nosferatu*!

Lee appeared in his first movie as the vampire Count in 1958. Since then, he has acted the role more times than anyone else — fourteen in all — and his handsome but coldhearted and cruel vampire has become most people's ideal Dracula.

▲ *The coldhearted Christopher Lee*

▼ *The ghoulish John Carradine*

A Medley of Monsters

All sorts of weird and wonderful vampire movies have been made over the years. Here are some from the 1960s — a western, a comedy and, to show they were still being made, a "proper" vampire chiller.

9.20am–10.49am

BILLY THE KID VS DRACULA

In this vampire western, famous gunslinger Billy the Kid (not the real one, of course) wants to retire peacefully with his sweetheart, ranch-owner Betty.

But before Billy can hang up his holster, he has to face a top-hatted Count Dracula, played by John Carradine (see p. 74).

Billy manages to do away with Dracula in the end, of course — although he uses a surgeon's scalpel in place of his trusty revolver!

Very silly, but a good laugh.

◀ *Christopher Lee in Dracula Prince of Darkness*

▶ *Ferdy Mayne as Count von Krolock in Dance of the Vampires*

11.00am–12.30pm

DRACULA PRINCE OF DARKNESS

Actor Christopher Lee returns, in a sequel to the 1958 *Dracula* which has very little to do with Bram Stoker's novel. The film gives the Count a loyal servant, Klove, who cuts the throat of a visitor to the castle over his master's grave. As the blood drips on to his remains, Dracula is resurrected.

Instead of Van Helsing, Dracula's opponent is an abbot, Father Sandor, who eventually destroys him by forcing him on to the broken ice of the castle moat and into the water below — according to the film, a sure-fire way to kill a vampire!

Fancy That

Christopher Lee didn't have many lines to learn for his role in *Dracula Prince of Darkness* — the Count doesn't utter a single word during the entire movie!

12.45pm–2.32pm

DANCE OF THE VAMPIRES

Accompanied by his cowardly assistant Alfred, vampire-hunter Professor Abronsius travels to Transylvania in pursuit of Count von Krolock, whom he suspects of being a bloodsucker!

The professor and Alfred's attempts to destroy the Count only make matters worse, and at the end of the film there's a hint that they, too, have now become vampires.

Funny *and* scary.

▲ *Grandpa and Eddie Munster*

Terror on Television

In the last 30 years, vampires haven't just kept themselves to the cinema, they've invaded our homes as well — on television that is! Here are a few of TV's top vampires.

2.45pm–4.15pm

THE MUNSTERS

Settle down for three half-hour episodes of the hit US comedy series from the 1960s. The monstrous Munster family includes Herman, who looks uncannily like Frankenstein's monster, his wife Lily, who's everyone's idea of the perfect female vampire, and Grandpa who's the spitting image of Count Dracula. And then there are the kids — Eddie the wolfboy and Marilyn.

The jokes are corny and the plots creaky — but you'll still laugh!

4.30pm–5.30pm

DARK SHADOWS

This marathon TV series ran for an amazing 1,225 episodes in the United States, between 1966 and 1971.

The plot revolves around the lives and loves of the wealthy, but rather bizarre Collins family, which includes a 175-year-old reluctant vampire called Barnabas — the undoubted star of the show.

Plenty of thrills, but the plot definitely ran out of steam towards the end of the series.

5.45pm–6.58pm

THE NIGHT STALKER

This TV film was a monster hit in its day. Nobody believes the hero (a scruffy reporter called Carl Kolchak) when he claims that a Transylvanian vampire is on the loose in Las Vegas — least of all the police. Kolchak is left with no choice but to pursue and destroy the killer alone.

A thrilling and genuinely scary movie.

7.10pm–7.30pm

COUNT DUCKULA

Chuckle at the cartoon adventures of the fang-less vegetarian vampire Count Duckula, his servants Igor and Nanny, and arch-enemy Dr Van Goosewing.

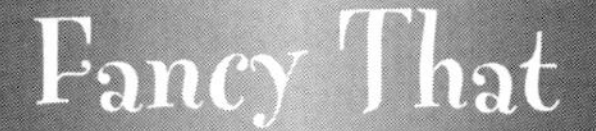

At least as strange as the Munsters were the stars of another hit 1960s US comedy series, *The Addams Family*. The show was re-made as a movie in 1991, starring Anjelica Huston as the vampire-like Morticia Addams. A sequel, *Addams Family Values*, was released in 1993.

QUEENS OF SCREAM

Unfortunately, in vampire films women are usually given far less toothsome parts than men — generally, they get attacked by vampires, scream a lot, and turn into vampires themselves!

BARBARA STEELE

★ ***(born 1938)*** ★

British-born Barbara Steele is the most successful horror-film actress in cinema history. She's appeared in more than 15 horror films, usually as a witch or a vampire. Sometimes she's played the role of the heroine, though, and in one film she was both the vampire and the vampire's victim!

▲ *Barbara Steel as a wide-eyed victim*

▲ *Ingrid Pitt prepares to pounce*

INGRID PITT

★ ***(born 1942)*** ★

Ingrid Pitt was born in Poland, and won fame in the 1970s for her portrayal of female vampires and wicked women in a series of British horror movies.

Her biggest role was as the evil Countess Báthory (see p. 60). Pitt's research for the part even included a visit to eastern Europe, to see the castle where the real Countess committed her horrible crimes.

Sinister Superstars

And finally, to bring things bang up to date, here's a pair of Hollywood vampire blockbusters from the 1990s — glamorous and gory and full of megastars.

Fancy That

Bram Stoker's Dracula cost more than US$40 million to make — that's nearly 100 times as much as the 1931 version!

▼ *Gary Oldman and Winona Ryder, stars of Bram Stoker's Dracula*

7.40pm–9.43pm

BRAM STOKER'S DRACULA

This spectacular film sticks quite closely to the plot of Bram Stoker's novel, with one main exception — in the film, Jonathan Harker's fiancée Mina Murray (played by Winona Ryder) actually falls in love with Dracula and helps to free him from his vampire curse so that he can die peacefully. In the book, of course, Mina is revolted by Dracula and helps to hunt him down.

The film is rather too long, but it does have some impressive special effects, particularly when Dracula (played by British actor Gary Oldman) turns into a hideous green monster — this happens whenever he gets cross, and is definitely nothing to do with the book!

▲ ***Kirsten Dunst, Brad Pitt and Tom Cruise — a trio of vampires***

10.00pm–12.01pm

INTERVIEW WITH THE VAMPIRE

Based on the best-selling book *Interview with the Vampire* by American Anne Rice, this movie recounts the adventures of vampire Louis de la Pointe Blanche (played by heart-throb Brad Pitt) and his fellow bloodsuckers — handsome but heartless Lestat (superstar Tom Cruise) and child-like Claudia (Kirsten Dunst).

The film moves from 18th-century New Orleans to modern-day San Francisco, where Louis tells the story of his long, unhappy life (or rather un-life) during an interview with a young man.

Louis explains how he was turned into a vampire by Lestat in 1791, and that he's doomed to an eternity of bloodsucking.

At the end of the film the young man is himself pounced on by Lestat, who's looking for a new vampire companion.

A slow-moving, but spectacular and often spooky movie.

- Vampire Hunter's Survival Guide
- Glossary
- Species List
- Index

VAMPIRE HUNTER'S SURVIVAL GUIDE

So now you know about all sorts of beastly bloodsuckers!
There are real ones, like mosquitoes and leeches,
and there are make-believe ones — mythical monsters like *Lilitu*,
and film and storybook vampires like Count Dracula.
But how much do you know about protecting yourself
against bloodsuckers, and most important
of all — how to destroy them if you're
ever unlucky enough to come across them?

VAMPIRE SPOTTER'S CHECKLIST

HANDY TIPS FOR DETERRING VAMPIRES AND OTHER BLOODSUCKERS

Crucifixes and crosses
Popular way of seeing off make-believe vampires, especially when worn around neck. In an emergency, can be improvised (for example, with two crossed swords or candlesticks).

Tar crosses painted on doors are quite useful against mythical blood-suckers in south-eastern Europe, as they get stuck to the tar and so cannot enter the house.

Knots and nets
Not generally much help against storybook and film vampires, but may be hung up in windows to stop a mythical blood-sucker like a Vrykolakas (see page 51) entering a house — it spends so long untying the knots, it has no time to attack.

Mosquito nets are very useful against insect bloodsuckers.

Seeds
Work in a similar way to knots and nets, as mythical bloodsuckers get obsessed with picking them up. Poppy and mustard seeds, and (in China) rice, are all thought effective.

Thorns
Also useful against mythical bloodsuckers, as the thorns catch on their shrouds and stop them from moving.

In Europe, hawthorn, dog rose and blackthorn are especially valued. Branches of these shrubs may be strewn around doors and windows, or put in graves.

GARLIC
Handy for putting off a wide range of make-believe vampires. Garlands of the stuff can be worn round the neck or hung up in houses. Pretty useless against animal bloodsuckers.

INSECT REPELLENT
Useful for keeping mosquitoes and other insect bloodsuckers away. Works against leeches if smeared on socks. Not much use against Dracula and his chums, though.

SURE-FIRE WAYS FOR DISPOSING OF UNWANTED BLOODSUCKERS

Burning to ashes
Very popular way of getting rid of make-believe vampires. Usually preceded by staking through heart and/or cutting off head.

Scattering the ashes over a wide area or throwing them in the river generally advisable.

DECAPITATION
Excellent way of dealing with make-believe vampires, especially if followed by burning to ashes.

Exposure to sunlight
Only of any use for getting rid of modern film or storybook vampires. Definitely not recommended when dealing with older storybook ones (especially Dracula), or mythical bloodsuckers.

Fly spray
Useful against many insect bloodsuckers, but entirely pointless against all make-believe vampires.

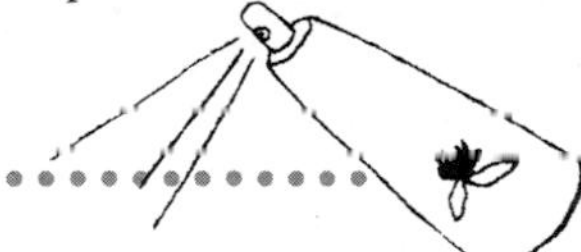

Fly swat
See **Fly spray**.

SILVER BULLET
Very occasionally used against make-believe vampires. Much more commonly applied against werewolves. Could be used against larger animal bloodsuckers (such as vampire bat), but extremely good aim needed, and in any case, method is very expensive!

STAKING THROUGH THE HEART
Most popular technique for destroying make-believe vampires. Stake should be made of ash, juniper or blackthorn wood, and single blow through the heart recommended. Protective clothing advised, as can be very messy. Usually followed by burning to ashes.

GLOSSARY

BUBONIC PLAGUE
A serious disease which has killed millions of people through history. If untreated, it usually results in death, even today. It is caused by a bacterium (germ) and is passed to humans mainly by fleas that live on infected rats.

LYME DISEASE
A disease that attacks humans. If untreated, it has unpleasant effects, including rashes, fevers and arthritis. It is caused by a bacterium, which is spread by infected deer ticks.

MAMMAL
A warm-blooded animal whose young feed on their mother's milk.

MYTHICAL
To do with folktales, myths and legends.

PARASITE
An animal or plant that for all or part of its life lives in or on a bigger animal or plant (called a host), feeding off it and usually harming it.

PROBOSCIS
The long tubular mouth-part through which some insects, including flies and butterflies, suck up liquid food.

A butterfly's proboscis

Biting insects such as mosquitoes have needle-like stylets hidden in their proboscis.

RABIES
A disease that attacks the brain of humans and other warm-blooded animals. If untreated, rabies victims usually die.

Rabies is caused by a virus (a microscopically tiny living thing which lives in another living thing's cells).

Because the virus is carried in saliva, it can be passed on when an infected animal bites another animal.

SALIVA
A liquid produced in the mouth of animals. Saliva aids digestion, mainly by wetting and softening food.

SLEEPING SICKNESS
A disease that attacks the nervous system of warm-blooded animals, and which usually results in death if untreated. It is caused by parasites, which are spread by biting insects.

SPECIES
A particular kind of animal or plant. Members of a species share the same body structure and basic features. Usually, only members of the same species can reproduce.

TEMPERATE
Regions between the tropics and poles, where summers are usually warm and wet, and winters, cool and wet.

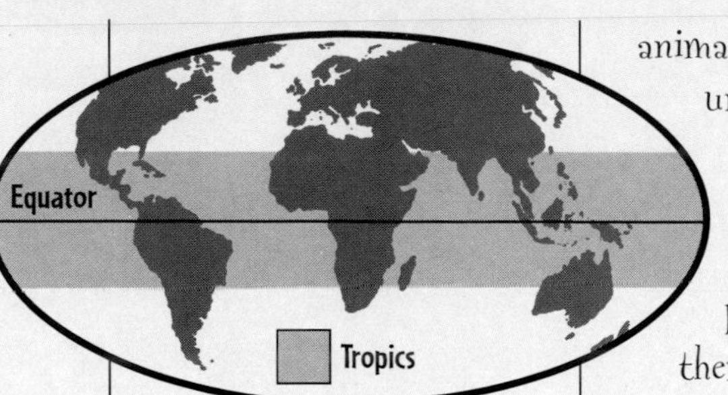

TROPICS
Regions near the Equator where the weather is mostly hot, and usually very rainy or very dry.

TYPHUS
A group of diseases that can infect warm-blooded animals and, if untreated, kill them. Lice, fleas, ticks or mites may all carry typhus parasites and pass them to other animals.

VAMPIRE
A mythical bloodsucker that is supposed to be dead, but which rises from its grave to kill its victims by sucking their blood, thereby turning them into vampires as well.

SPECIES LIST

Anopheles mosquitoes	*Anopheles* species
blue-footed booby	*Sula nebouxii*
common vampire bat	*Desmodus rotundus*
deer ticks	*Ixodes* species
European medicinal leech	*Hirudo medicinalis*
giant Amazonian horse-leech	*Haementaria ghiliani*
head louse	*Pediculus humanus capitis*
human flea	*Pulex irritans*
river lamprey	*Lampetra fluviatilis*
sharp-beaked ground finch	*Geospiza difficilis*
tsetse flies	*Glossina* species

INDEX

F

G

H

I

K

L

M

N

O

P

R

S

T

U

V

W

ACKNOWLEDGEMENTS

PHOTOGRAPHS

ARDEA London Ltd: Pascal Goetgheluck 40b; Adrian Warren 25b.
Bruce Coleman Ltd: Dieter & Mary Plage 28t; Hans Reinhard 43; Gunter Ziesler 25t.
J. S. Library International: 42.
The Kobal Collection: 72–73; CBS/MCA/Universal 78t, 78–79; Embassy 68l; Geffen Pictures 82; Hammer 68r, 75t; Hammer/20th C. Fox 76; Hammer/AIP 80tr; Hammer/Universal 73t, 73b; MGM 77; Panda Film 80bl; Paramount (Firooz Zahedi) 22, 79; Frana-Film GMBH, Berlin 70; Universal 22, 71, 74, 74–75; Zoetrope/Columbia Tri-Star 81.
Kunsthistorisches Museum, Vienna/Bridgeman Art Library: MAM68944 00307 Vlad the Impaler (Vlad VI of Wallachia) (died 1462), German School (16th century) 45br.
NHPA: G. I. Bernard 21, 38; Stephen Dalton 26, 33; Daniel Heuclin 39b.
Oxford Scientific Films: Mike Birkhead 31; Scott Camazine 39t; Dr. F. Köster 28b, 29; Tim Shepherd 36.
Planet Earth Pictures: Paulo de Oliveira 40t
Warner Bros./BFI Stills Department: "The Mark of the Vampire" © 1935 Turner Entertainment Co. 65.
ZEFA: 35.

ILLUSTRATIONS

John Burns (Bardon Cartoon Agents): 5–20.
Maxine Hamil: 26, 29, 33t, 38, 39, 40, 43.
Axel Scheffler: 45–64, 89–91.
Sue Shields: 4.
Holly Swain: 83–87, 92.
Ian Thompson: 22, 23, 27, 32, 33b, 34, 35b, 37, 41, 44.

COVER

Jonathan Hair: design
Luis Rey: illustration

CREDITS

Designed by
Beth Aves
Edited by
Jackie Gaff

First published 1998
by Walker Books Ltd
87 Vauxhall Walk
London SE11 5HJ

This edition published
2000

10 9 8 7 6 5 4 3 2 1

Printed in Hong Kong

British Library Cataloguing in Publication Data: a catalogue record for this book is available from the British Library.

ISBN 0-7445-7711-X